Save the Planet

Let's Recycle

Claire Llewellyn

First published in the UK in 2003 by
Chrysalis Children's Books
An imprint of Chrysalis Books Group Plc
The Chrysalis Building
Bramley Road
London W10 6SP

Paperback edition first published in 2005

ISBN 1-84138-691-X (hb)
ISBN 1-84458-304-X (pb)

British Library Cataloguing in Publication Data
for this book is available from the British Library.

Editorial Manager: Joyce Bentley
Senior Editor: Sarah Nunn
Design: Stonecastle Graphics Ltd
Illustrations: Paul B. Davies
Picture researcher: Paul Turner

Printed in China

10 9 8 7 6 5 4 3 2 1

Picture credits:
Alcan:
page 21 (centre left).
Garden & Wildlife Matters Photo Library:
pages 4 © John Feltwell/Garden Matters (right),
15 © John Feltwell/Garden Matters (below).
Pilkington plc:
pages 16, 18 (below).
Roddy Paine Photographic Studios:
pages 4 (left), 5, 6 (top), 27.
Sylvia Cordaiy Photo Library:
pages 18 (top), 26.

Contents

What is recycling?

Recycling means using old **materials** to make new things. For example, it means using the paper in old magazines to make new paper tissues, notepads and bags.

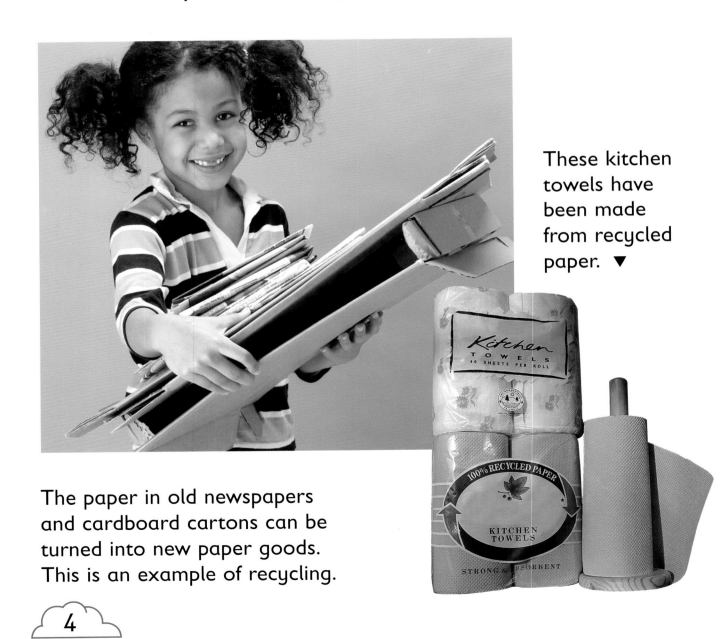

These kitchen towels have been made from recycled paper. ▼

The paper in old newspapers and cardboard cartons can be turned into new paper goods. This is an example of recycling.

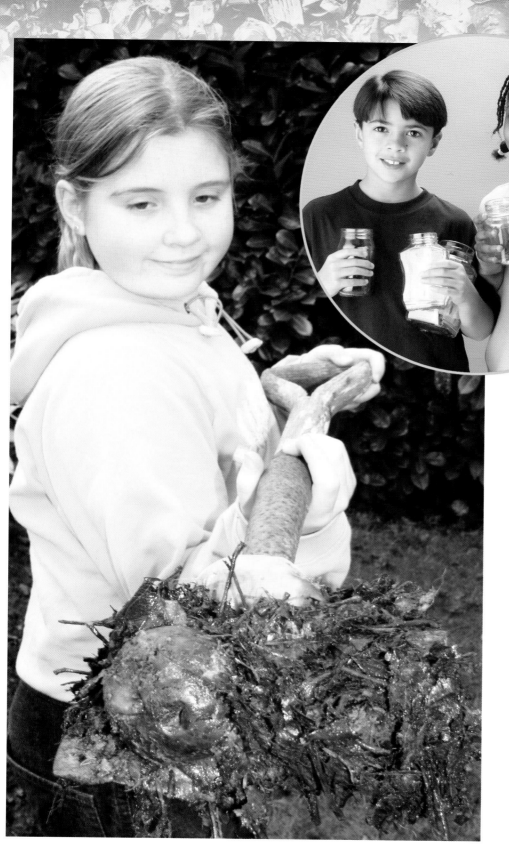

▲
Recycling
means using
the glass in
old jars to
make brand
new bottles.

◄
Garden waste
and fruit and
vegetable
peelings can
be recycled
into **compost**.

5

What a waste!

Every week, we throw a lot of rubbish away. Most of this rubbish is made of useful materials, which could be recycled.

When our rubbish is taken away, valuable materials, such as metal and glass, are lost for ever.

Stop! The glass in this jar could be recycled. Throwing it away is a waste.

This is what we throw away
every week. Is it really rubbish?

Glass bottles
and jars.

Rags and
old clothes.

Metal cans
and tins.

Plastic
bottles
and cartons.

Newspapers,
leaflets, old
envelopes,
old cards
and food
packaging.

Food scraps,
vegetable
peelings, dead
flowers and
other **organic
waste**.

Where does the rubbish go?

Most of our rubbish is dumped in huge holes in the ground called **landfill sites**. There, the rubbish slowly begins to rot. This produces nasty **gases** and poisonous **liquids**, which trickle into the water supply deep underground.

Landfill sites are dirty and spoil the **environment**. We will not need so many of them if we throw less rubbish away.

Some rubbish is burned in **incinerators**. This makes smoke that **pollutes** the air, and is harmful for us to breathe.

Getting rid of rubbish

Most of us don't want to think about our rubbish, we just want it to disappear. Look carefully at the picture below. Can you see why our bins are so full? What is being thrown away?

Every bin in the street is full up. This family has so much rubbish, it has filled an extra bag!

These old newspapers are going in the bin. They contain useful paper.

There is lots of useful metal in these tins and cans but they are being thrown out too.

Empty glass bottles are being thrown away. They contain useful glass.

These "old" clothes don't fit any more, but they look as good as new.

These vegetable peelings could be made into compost for the garden.

11

A better way with rubbish

There are other ways of getting rid of rubbish without throwing it in the bin. Can you see what they are in this picture? If every dustbin was as empty as these, we would need fewer landfill sites.

The rubbish is being sorted before it goes into the bin.

Organic waste goes into the compost bin.

Everything made of paper is put in this box.

All the glass is put in this box.

Everything that can be recycled is taken to nearby **recycling points**.

There is very little rubbish in the bin.

Old clothes are given to charity shops.

All the tins and cans go in this box.

Gathering raw materials

All the goods we buy and which, in time, we throw away are made from wood, metal, rock, oil and other **raw materials**. These are hard to gather. It takes a lot of hard work, powerful machines and a huge amount of **fuel**.

Paper is made from trees. The trees are cut down, put onto trucks, and driven along roads to paper mills.

▲ Rocks and minerals are the materials from which we make glass and many metals. It takes lots of **energy** to dig them out of the ground.

Digging, chopping and building ▶ work spoils the environment. It destroys the **habitats** of animals and plants.

Using raw materials

Wood, rocks and oil are taken to factories. Here, more machines get to work on them, changing them into useful materials such as paper, glass and plastic. This takes a lot of energy, which comes from burning fuel.

Sand and rock have to be crushed and then heated to make glass.

Wooden logs have to be chopped up and soaked in water before they can be made into paper.

Fuels for ever?
Factories burn coal, gas and oil to get energy for their machines. These fuels won't last for ever. We need to use them carefully.

Factories burn huge amounts of fuel. This makes smoke that pollutes the air.

Don't throw away – recycle!

When we throw something away, we waste the material and energy that were used to make it. Recycling is so much better. Recycling saves energy and takes fewer raw materials from the Earth.

Recycling glass is much easier than making it from raw materials. First, glass bottles are sorted, cleaned and crushed.

Next, the crushed glass is heated till it melts. This takes a lot less energy than melting sand and rock!

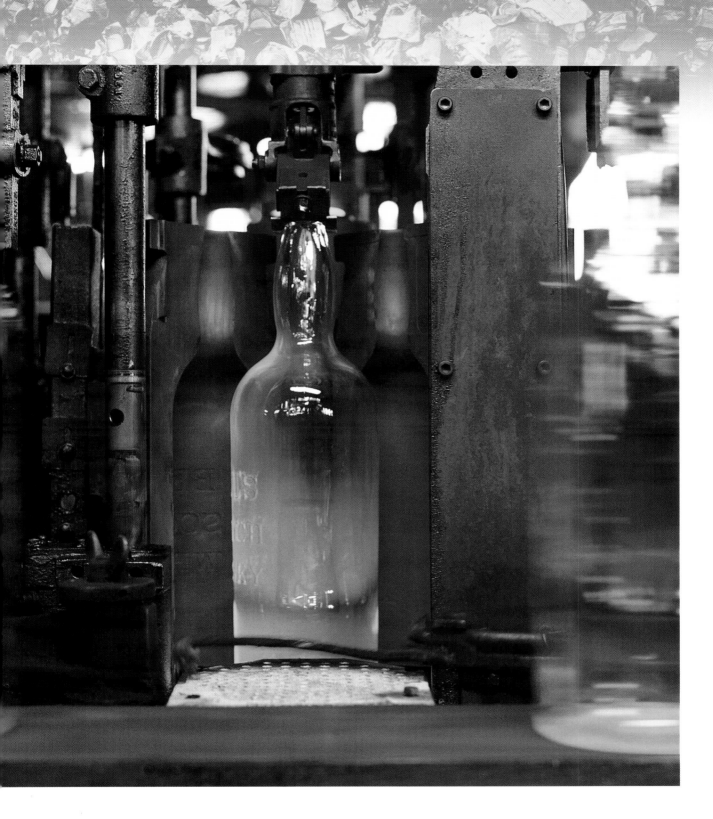

Then the hot glass is shaped
into new bottles and jars.

Old rubbish, new materials

Just as glass can be recycled, so can paper, **aluminium**, steel, and some plastics. It takes far less energy to recycle these materials than to make them from scratch.

Old paper is chopped up and added to water to make new recycled paper.

Aluminium drinks cans are crushed and heated to make new sheets of aluminium.

Plastic is not very easy to recycle, but some kinds can be used to make flower pots, furniture, traffic cones and even fleece jackets.

Going shopping

Some of the goods we buy in the shops waste energy and raw materials. Have a look at the picture below. Can you see how careless shopping adds to the rubbish in our bins?

These plastic bottles are very small. They will not last long.

This fruit has a lot of packaging. It will all end up in the bin.

Plastic bottles and other containers are usually thrown away when they are finished.

The paper in these tissues has been made from wood.

This shopper has lots of thin plastic bags. They will end up as rubbish.

A better way of shopping

A wise shopper can cut down on waste. Look at the picture below. Can you see how people are saving energy and materials? This will mean less rubbish in their bin!

This big plastic bottle will last for years. Refills come in paper cartons, which cuts out the need for extra plastic.

This fruit is loose. It needs very little packaging – just a paper bag.

These tissues are made from recycled paper. This uses less energy than tissues made from wood.

This shopping bag is very strong. It can be used over and over again.

These bottles are made of recycled glass. Glass is a better choice than plastic because it is easier to recycle.

Always look for this sign on the goods you buy. It shows they are made from recyclable materials.

Small steps, big results

Recycling your rubbish is a small step, so will it make a difference? Of course, it will! If your step is copied by millions of other people, the results for the Earth will be huge! Everyone shares the planet. Everyone can help to save it.

What would happen if everyone recycled their rubbish?

If everyone was good at recycling we wouldn't have so much rubbish to get rid of. There would be fewer incinerators and landfill sites. This would be good for the environment.

We would use fewer raw materials. This would save energy and protect wildlife habitats.

Factories would produce more recycled goods. This would save energy and cut the air pollution that comes from burning fuel.

Over to you!

Some places have laws to make people recycle. Other places do not. No one wants to see mountains of rubbish. Why not try one of the ideas below, and help to get people recycling?

Make posters to encourage people to recycle their rubbish. Think of a clever slogan like "Slim your bin!", "Re-think rubbish" or "Waste wise". Stick a poster on your bin or in your home, school or library.

For one week, keep a record of everything that your family throws away. Highlight things that could have been recycled. Pin up your record for everyone to see.

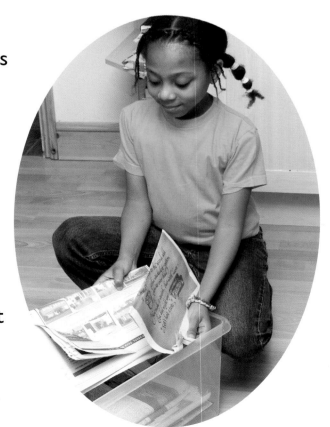

Suggest that your parents have different bins for paper, glass, metal and plastics, and offer to sort the rubbish.

Have you got room for a compost bin? Use it to store organic waste and in a few months you'll have compost to put on all your plants.

Do a survey to find out how many people in your class or school regularly recycle their rubbish.

Are there plenty of recycling points in your town? Are there any at your school? If not, complain! Write to your paper or talk to your teacher.

Does your school use recycled paper? If not, try and make them change their mind.

With a grown-up, sort out your old clothes, toys and books and give them to friends, charity shops or jumble sales.

Join a group that helps to protect the environment. Two of the groups you could try are:
Friends of the the Earth www.foe.co.uk
Greenpeace www.greenpeace.org.uk

Glossary

Aluminium A grey metal that is very light. It is used to make foil, cans and many other things.

Compost The crumbly mixture we add to soil to help plants to grow. Compost is decayed organic waste.

Energy The power that makes machines and living things able to work. We can get energy from burning fuels.

Environment The land, air and sea that make up the world around us.

Fuel Wood, coal, oil or some other material that can be burned for heat and power.

Gas A substance like air that is not solid or liquid. Air is a mixture of different gases.

Habitat The natural home of an animal or plant.

Incinerator A machine that is used to burn unwanted things.

Landfill site A huge hole in the ground where rubbish is buried.

Liquid A substance like water that runs and flows.

Material Something like wood, metal, plastic or glass that is used to make different things.

Organic waste Any waste, such as dead flowers or vegetable peelings, that is natural and comes from plants.

Packaging The wrapping that is used to pack foods and other things we buy.

Pollute To spoil the air, land or water with harmful substances.

Raw material A natural material that is the starting point for making something new. Oil is the raw material that is used to make plastic.

Recycle To take an old material and use it again to make something new.

Recycling point A place where recyclable materials can be taken and deposited, ready for collection.

Index